FOLLOWING A FAITH

A HINDU life

Cath Senker

W
FRANKLIN WATTS

Franklin Watts
Published in paperback in Great Britain in 2019 by
The Watts Publishing Group

Credits
Series Editor: Amy Pimperton/Julia Bird
Series Designer: Krina Patel

Consultant: Rasamandala Das, ISKCON Educational Services

ISBN 978 1 4451 5804 4

Picture credits: agefotostock/Alamy: 14. Olesia Agudova/Shutterstock: back
cover bg. Amateurs/Shutterstock: 10. Anandoart/Dreamstime: 12. Viacheslav
Belyaev /Dreamstime: 2, 25b. Parthkumar Bhatt/Dreamstime: 8b. Nilanjan
Bhattacharya/Dreamstime: 26. A J Cassaigne/Photononstop/Superstock: 16t. Roop
Dey/Shutterstock: 24t. diy13/Shutterstock: 28. Patrice Duforets/Dreamstime:
29b. Louise Batalla Duran/Alamy: 7, 18. espies/Shutterstock: 13b, 24b. Dmitrijs
Gerciks/Dreamstime: 9b. Godong/Robert Harding PL: 13t. Geoff Goldswain/Alamy:
20, 31. JOAT/Shutterstock: 8t, 32. Muslim Kapasi/Dreamstime: 25t. Claudine
Van Massenhove/Shutterstock: 5t. Gideon Mendel/Getty Images: 6. MoLarjung/
Shutterstock: 29t. Thaweesak Nammaneewong/123RF: front cover c, 1. Nila
Newson/Dreamstime: 5b. Apidech Ninkhlai/Dreamstime: 17. norriko/Shutterstock:
11b. NuPhoto/Getty Images: 9t. Naynesh Parmar/Dreamstime: 27b. Sohel Parvez/
Shutterstock: 23 main. David Pearson/Alamy: 21. Picstudio/Dreamstime: 11t. pjhpix/
Shutterstock: 4. Nagesh Rao/CC Wikimedia: 19. Samrat35/Dreamstime: 27t. Dipak
Shelare/Shutterstock: back cover tl & tr, 23 inset. Val Shevchenko/Shutterstock:
front cover main. © Shree Ghanapathy Temple: 15b. Steve Speller/Alamy: 15t.
TheLightPainter/Shutterstock: 22. Wikimedia Commons: 16b.

The author and publishers would like to thank the following people or
organisations whose material is included in this book: Gadadhara Pandit
Dasa: p.11; Archit Asthana: p.27;

Franklin Watts
An imprint of
Hachette Children's Group
Part of The Watts Publishing Group
Carmelite House
50 Victoria Embankment
London EC4Y 0DZ

An Hachette UK Company
www.hachette.co.uk
www.franklinwatts.co.uk

Printed in Dubai

MIX
Paper from
responsible sources
FSC® C104740

CONTENTS

WHAT DOES IT MEAN TO BE A HINDU?

One of the oldest faiths in the world, Hinduism began in India at least five thousand years ago. More than 90 per cent of Hindus still live there now. Other communities are found all around the world. Hinduism is more a way of life than a religion – acting in the right way is more important than following particular customs.

BRAHMAN

Hinduism is a rich and varied religion, embracing a wide variety of ideas and beliefs. Most Hindus believe in one God – Brahman, the Supreme Being, who is everywhere. Hindus believe that the soul or 'real self' (*atman*) is also brahman (eternal spirit). This atman is present in all forms of life.

FORMS OF GOD

Hindus worship God (Brahma) in many forms. The three most important forms are the Trimurti, three deities who represent different aspects of God. These are Brahma the creator, Vishnu the protector and Shiva the destroyer. Each of these three has a goddess wife. Vishnu and Shiva appear in many forms, and most Hindus are devoted to one of them, or to one of the goddesses.

Some deities have many arms and faces. Brahma, the creator, (left) has four faces to look north, south, east and west all at the same time.

HINDU LIFE

Hindus are brought up in the faith. They learn from their parents, performing *puja* (worship) at home and going to the mandir, the Hindu temple. Holy books, including the *Vedas* and the *Bhagavad Gita*, teach them how to worship God and to live their lives as best they can. Every year, Hindu communities celebrate religious festivals. Some mark key events, such as the birth of a Hindu deity. Other gatherings mark the rites of passage through life, from birth to marriage to death.

DHARMA

Hindus believe that everyone has their own *dharma*, or duty, in life that they should fulfil. For a young person, dharma includes being a good student and respecting their parents.

BORN INTO THE HINDU FAITH

Hindu rituals start even before birth. Halfway through a woman's pregnancy, family members go to the mandir to pray that the child will be healthy and happy. The mother reads prayers from the holy books to her unborn baby.

NAMING A BABY

On the twelfth day after the birth, the naming ceremony traditionally takes place. The parents consult with a priest to choose a name that will bring the child good luck. He uses Hindu astrology to work out a suitable name, depending on exactly when and where the baby was born. Hindus are often given a name linked to a god or goddess.

The naming ceremony is called namakaran.

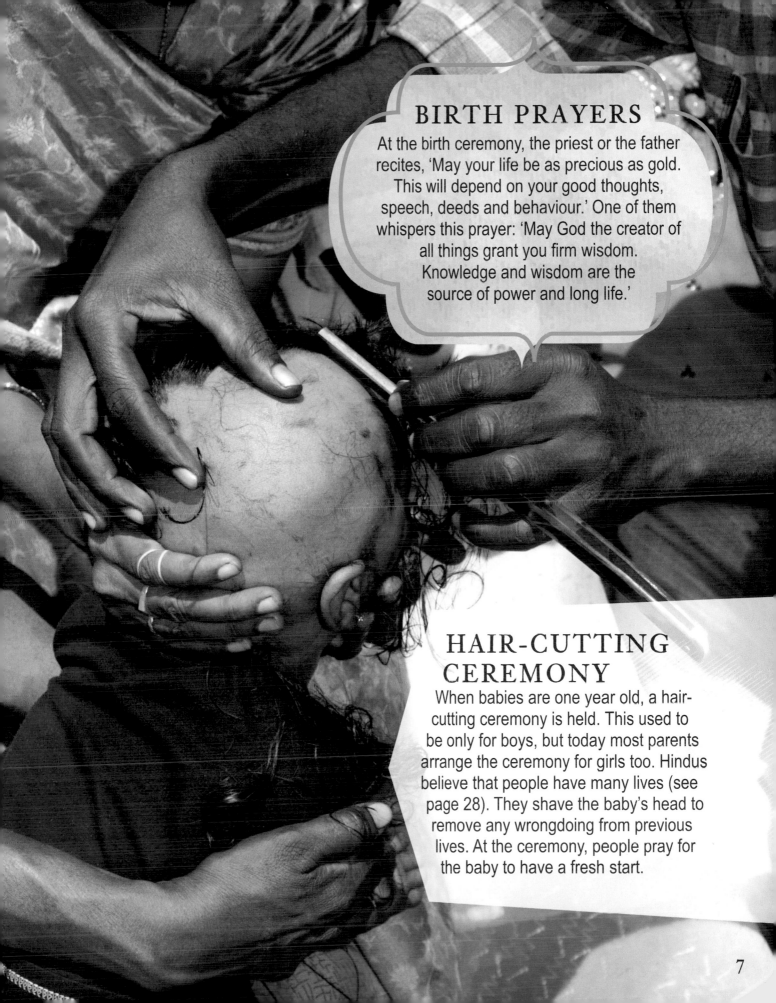

BIRTH PRAYERS

At the birth ceremony, the priest or the father recites, 'May your life be as precious as gold. This will depend on your good thoughts, speech, deeds and behaviour.' One of them whispers this prayer: 'May God the creator of all things grant you firm wisdom. Knowledge and wisdom are the source of power and long life.'

HAIR-CUTTING CEREMONY

When babies are one year old, a hair-cutting ceremony is held. This used to be only for boys, but today most parents arrange the ceremony for girls too. Hindus believe that people have many lives (see page 28). They shave the baby's head to remove any wrongdoing from previous lives. At the ceremony, people pray for the baby to have a fresh start.

GROWING UP

As they grow up, Hindu children mostly learn about their faith at home, taking part in daily worship. They visit the mandir to study Hinduism and explore their culture further.

SHRINES

According to Hinduism, God is everywhere so followers can perform puja and worship God anywhere, at any time. Most families have their own shrine at home. On the shrine are *murtis* – sacred statues that represent the gods and goddesses. Hindus believe that God is present in the murti, or even as the murti.

Ganesh, the elephant god, is believed to solve problems.

PERFORMING PUJA

Hindus wash so they are clean for puja. They light some incense, say prayers and make offerings of sweets or fruit to the murtis. Worshippers may bathe the murti with milk and water and dress it. Sometimes, they mark their own forehead with kumkum paste, a symbol of spiritual wisdom. Then they perform the arti ceremony (see page 13).

HINDU CULTURE

Children find out about Hinduism outside the home, too. They may go to special classes at the mandir to study their family's Indian language. There are many languages spoken in India, such as Gujarati and Punjabi, so the language they learn depends on where in India their family comes from. The young people read stories from the holy books, such as the *Ramayana* (see page 17), and recite prayers. To discover their culture, they may join traditional Indian dance classes or learn to play the tabla, sitar or other traditional Indian musical instruments.

A GOOD HINDU

Grandparents and parents teach children how to be good Hindus. Among other things, they teach them to:

- tell the truth
- be honest and not to steal
- know the difference between right and wrong
- have faith in God
- be kind towards all creation – both people and animals.

CHANTING AUM

Aum is a sacred symbol that stands for Brahman. Hindus chant the word 'aum' as a mantra, or prayer. It is a sacred sound and is perhaps the most important Hindu mantra.

FOOD AND FASTING

Many Hindus are vegetarians and bring up their children to avoid eating meat, fish and eggs. They believe that the real self (atman) is in all living things and it is therefore wrong to kill and eat animals.

COWS

To Hindus, the cow is a particularly holy animal because it provides milk. Dairy foods such as milk are vital to Hindus since they are usually vegetarian. In India, cows wander freely in the streets. Devout Hindus – even if they eat some meat – will never eat beef.

OFFERINGS

Since most Hindus live in India or their family is Indian, they often eat traditional dishes from their homeland – vegetable curries, *chapattis* (round, flat bread) and lentil *dhal*. Before eating, people may make a food offering at their shrine. The holy book, the *Bhagavad Gita*, says people should offer food to the popular deity Krishna (see page 22–23) before eating.

VEGETARIANISM

A Hindu in the USA explains why it is important to be vegetarian: 'Animals live and care for each other as much as humans do. They will do whatever they can to defend their family members. They suffer emotionally when their offspring are taken away from them. How is it that we can be so callous (uncaring) towards these creatures of God?'
(Gadadhara Pandit Dasa)

FASTING

At festivals, Hindus fast (go without food) to show their devotion to God. Some people eat nothing at all during the fast, while others only have simple dishes with milk, yoghurt and fruit. They avoid heavier foods, such as rice, grains, flour, lentils and some spices. Hindus believe fasting clears the mind so they can focus on prayer and reading holy books.

WORSHIP AT THE MANDIR

One of the best things about following a faith is being part of a community. Hindus go regularly to their mandir or temple. These vary from magnificent, specially built buildings to small houses. At the mandir, Hindus worship, discuss community matters, eat together and meditate.

MURTIS

When they arrive, Hindus remove their shoes, as they do when entering any building. They ring a bell to tell the deities they are present. In the main hall are murtis. Each mandir is dedicated to a deity – often Vishnu or Lakshmi. A large murti of that god or goddess stands on the main shrine. Often there are smaller shrines with other deities at the sides. The worshippers bow down in front of the murtis to honour them and make offerings of flowers, money and cooking ingredients.

ARTI

A priest leads the service at the mandir. A central part is the welcoming arti ceremony. After lighting the *diva* lamps on the arti tray, the priest moves the tray slowly in a circle in front of the main deity to offer love and respect. He may also offer items such as incense, flowers or a fan. Then he offers the tray to the worshippers, who place some coins on it. To receive blessings, people hold their hands over the flame and then bring their hands over their forehead. As the tray goes around, worshippers sing a hymn and chant a prayer, accompanied by musicians playing the harmonium, drums and cymbals.

PRASHAD

At the end of puja, the worshippers receive *prashad*. This is usually fruit, nuts or sweets. Prashad is a symbol of the give and take between worshippers and God and is seen to purify the worshippers' body and mind. Once the offerings to the deities have been made, they are considered sacred and especially pure. Some of the offerings are returned to the worshippers, bringing them God's blessings. Afterwards, the worshippers eat a meal together.

HELPING THE COMMUNITY

The mandir is at the heart of the Hindu community. It is the duty of the mandir priest or priests to care for the murtis, as well as to lead puja (worship). Every day, the priest washes and dresses the murtis and makes food offerings.

A PRIEST'S ROLE

The priest assists his community throughout the cycle of life. He blesses newborn babies and marries couples. When people have questions, he explains Hindu customs and their meaning, and he helps if they have difficulties in their life. When someone dies, the priest recites mantras and comforts the grieving family.

GIVING TO OTHERS

It is a vital part of dharma – religious duty – for adult Hindus to assist their community. Acts of giving and charity are called *dana*. Naturally, people's first duty is to their own family. Traditionally, elderly relatives are looked after by the wider family. Dana extends beyond the family too, and Hindus often do charitable work and donate money to good causes. At the mandir, people hold events to raise money for the wider community. They might fundraise to help towns or villages in India that are affected by natural disasters, such as earthquakes, for example.

A family group goes together to a mandir in Gujarat, India.

COMMUNITY FOCUS

Based in west London, volunteers from the Shree Ghanapathy Temple cook a delicious Indian meal for homeless people in central London every Sunday. Their volunteer drivers also work with social services, taking meals to elderly and disabled people. The children at the mandir collect spare toys and books to give to a centre that works with children in need. Mandir members do conservation work too – planting trees and helping to clear and maintain a section of local land by the river.

HOLY BOOKS

Hindu beliefs and customs are based on their scriptures – their holy books. They are mostly written in the ancient Indian language of Sanskrit. Some people study Sanskrit so they can read the original texts for themselves.

SPOKEN WORD

There are two kinds of scriptures. *Shruti* are 'heard' scriptures. Hindus believe that wise men in ancient times both heard God's words and felt them from within. The second type is *Smriti* – 'remembered'. Both Shruti and Smriti scriptures were passed on by word of mouth for centuries until eventually, they were written down.

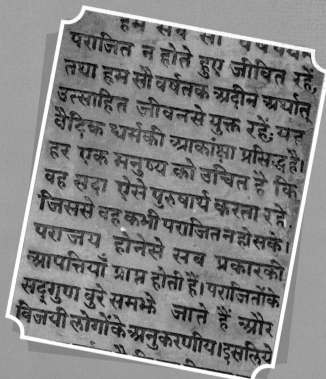

A section from the Hindu scriptures, written in Sanskrit.

SHRUTI SCRIPTURES

The Shruti texts include the *Vedas. Veda* means 'knowledge' or 'wisdom'. These are some of the oldest Hindu scriptures. Written down between 1200 and 1000 BCE, they contain hymns, stories and poems about God. Another set are the *Upanishads. Upanishad* literally means 'near-down-sit'. Groups of young men and spiritual teachers used to sit discussing the nature of the universe and why humans are here on Earth. The ideas that arose from the discussions were written down – about God, the self and the world itself.

A wooden carving of a scene from the Ramayana

SMRITI STORIES

Shruti texts were hard for most people to understand, so stories were told to explain the ideas of Hinduism in a simple way and show how to apply them in daily life. These are the Smriti scriptures. They include the two histories – the *Mahabharata* and the *Ramayana*. They are both extraordinarily long – the *Mahabharata* has almost 100,000 verses and includes the *Bhagavad Gita*, one of the most important Hindu texts. The *Ramayana* tells the famous story of Rama and Sita (see page 25). The Smriti scriptures also include the 18 *Puranas*, which describe the creation of the universe and the first men, among other things.

THE BHAGAVAD GITA

In one verse from the *Bhagavad Gita*, the god Krishna explains that the value of the offerings people make to the deities is not the main thing – it's the love in their hearts with which they give them: 'Whoever offers me a leaf, a flower, a fruit or water with devotion, that offer of devotion I will accept from the pure of heart.'

SACRED THREAD CEREMONY

Some Hindu boys aged between 7 and 14 begin to learn Sanskrit so they can read and study the holy books. Their families hold the sacred thread ceremony to celebrate this rite of passage. In some communities, girls also have the ceremony, but do not usually receive and wear the sacred thread.

THREE THREADS, THREE VOWS

The sacred thread ceremony takes place at home, with friends, family and the priest. It is quite a challenge for the boy, who has to recite a verse from the first *Veda* in Sanskrit in front of an audience. He promises to carry out his duties to the deities, his ancestors and the saints and seers. The priest gives the boy a loop of cotton thread, made from three strands, which stand for three vows (promises): to respect knowledge, his parents and society. The child puts the thread on over his left shoulder, across his chest and under his right arm.

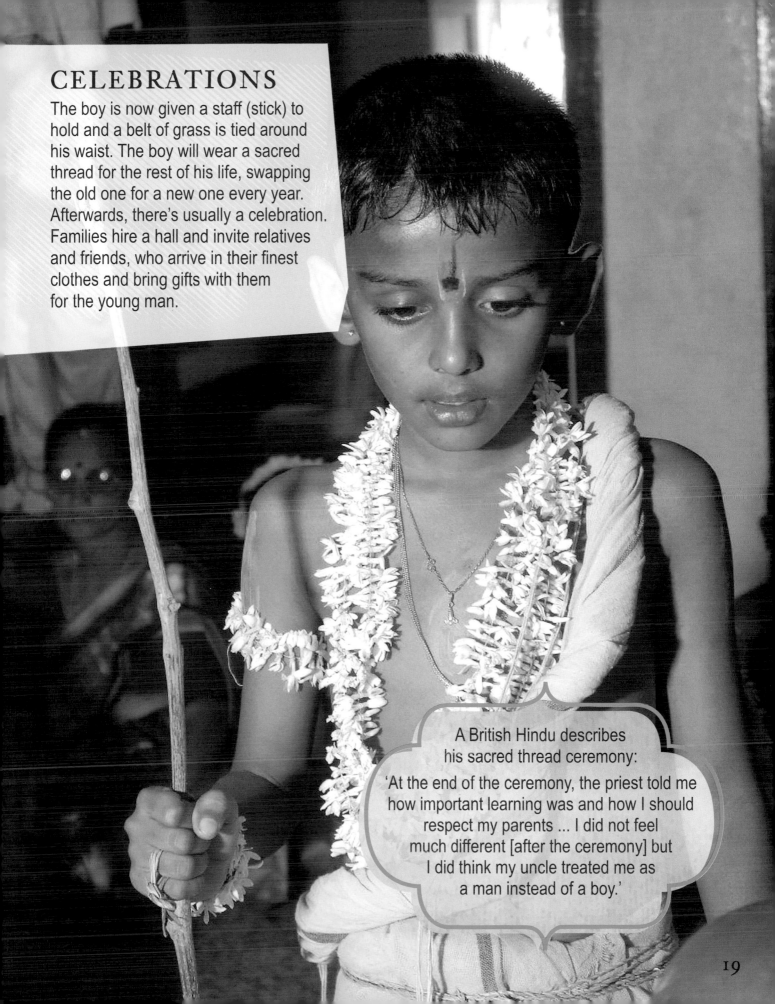

CELEBRATIONS

The boy is now given a staff (stick) to hold and a belt of grass is tied around his waist. The boy will wear a sacred thread for the rest of his life, swapping the old one for a new one every year. Afterwards, there's usually a celebration. Families hire a hall and invite relatives and friends, who arrive in their finest clothes and bring gifts with them for the young man.

A British Hindu describes his sacred thread ceremony:

'At the end of the ceremony, the priest told me how important learning was and how I should respect my parents ... I did not feel much different [after the ceremony] but I did think my uncle treated me as a man instead of a boy.'

WEDDING CELEBRATIONS

The next major stage in Hindu life is marriage. For Hindus, it is considered a duty to marry and have children. A wedding is a special occasion that brings together two families and their communities. Often, it is a huge event.

SACRED PLACE

The wedding may be held in a hall or garden. A sacred place with a canopy is set up – Hindus believe the canopy keeps the good energy inside. The bride sits in the sacred place, usually dressed in a beautiful red sari. Red is seen as a symbol of purity, but also of happiness. The groom and his family enter the hall, singing and dancing.

At their wedding, the bride and groom are treated like a king and queen for a day.

SEVEN STEPS, SEVEN WISHES

Under the canopy, the priest lights the holy fire and the couple sit in front of it. The priest ties the end of the bride's sari to the groom's scarf – a symbol that they are being joined together. While the priest recites prayers, the couple make offerings of rice and ghee to the fire. They walk around the fire four times. For the first three rounds, the groom leads, for the fourth, the bride. Now comes the most significant part. The couple take seven steps together and make seven wishes, while the priest recites mantras from the *Vedas*. The pair are now married.

RELIGIOUS RITUALS

The wedding rituals symbolise the couple's love for each other and their union, and they are intended to protect the couple from harm. Afterwards, the guests throw flower petals and rice over the pair for good luck, and offer gifts. The ceremony is followed by a lavish feast.

MARRIAGE MANTRA

Here are the seven steps in the Asvalayana Grihya Sutra, the Marriage Mantra: 'Take the first step for food, take the second step for strength, the third for prosperity [wealth], the fourth for happiness, the fifth for children ... Take the sixth step for seasonal pleasures, take the seventh step for friendship.'

21

KRISHNA JANMASHTAMI

As well as family celebrations, there are also religious festivals, fixed according to the Hindu lunar calendar. In August or September, Krishna Janmashtami celebrates the birth of Krishna. For some Hindus, it is the most important festival.

HAPPY BIRTHDAY KRISHNA!

On the eve of Krishna's birth, people assemble at the mandir. It has been brightly decorated, and the murtis of Krishna and his companions are dressed in festive clothes. The priest reads from the scriptures and tells stories about Krishna. Everyone sings *bhajans* – holy songs. Hindus believe Krishna was born at midnight, so everyone eagerly awaits the moment. Children get very excited!

AVATARS

Krishna is one of the avatars of Vishnu, and he is one of the most popular gods. You may know the word 'avatar' from the online world, but it actually comes from a Hindu word that means a god who comes to Earth in human form. Hindus believe that Vishnu protects the universe. Sometimes he has to appear on Earth as an avatar to restore order.

FOOD AND FUN

At midnight, bells are rung to celebrate Krishna's birth and there is a beautiful arti ceremony. A murti of baby Krishna in a crib is revealed, and children may take it in turns to rock the murti. People recite prayers and make offerings of dairy foods – Krishna's favourites – such as butter and desserts made with milk. Many worshippers have fasted all day so they are really hungry. After puja, they share some of the offerings or sit down for a full meal.

After the ceremony at the mandir, people perform plays about Krishna and enjoy traditional dancing.

DAHI HANDI

Dahi Handi is celebrated in the cities of Mumbai and Pune during Krishna Janmashtami. It remembers how much Lord Krishna loved to eat freshly made butter. His mother and aunts had to hide it in a pot out of his reach! At Dahi Handi, boys form a human pyramid to try to reach and break an earthen pot of butter – just as Krishna did.

DIWALI – FESTIVAL OF LIGHT

Diwali is a major Hindu festival, held in October or November. At this time, people remember the story of Rama and Sita in the *Ramayana*.

LOVE AND LIGHT

At home, people light diva lamps in every room. The divas are a symbol of good (light) defeating evil (darkness) at the end of the tale. Beautiful coloured patterns called *rangoli* are made to welcome Lakshmi, the goddess of wealth. In India, people make rangolis on their doorstep, using rice powder, coloured chalks, lentils or beads. They hope Lakshmi will visit and bring them good luck in the year to come.

Rangoli

FUN AND FIREWORKS

At the mandir, divas are lit around the shrine. There is music and traditional dancing, and a vegetarian feast with curries, dhal and yoghurt. For dessert, people enjoy *jalebi* (sweet shapes made of fried dough and syrup) or *kheer* – Indian rice pudding. Some Hindu communities hold big parties. In Sydney, Australia, a model of Ravana (the evil demon in the story) is set on fire at sunset. Later, there is a huge firework display, lighting up the night sky.

Firework displays are held on the main day of the Diwali festival.

Deities of Rama and Sita in a mandir.

RAMA AND SITA

Prince Rama expected to become king after his father. But his stepmother insisted that her own son should become king instead. She forced the king to send Rama and his wife Sita far away. They lived in the deep forest for 14 years. One day, the demon king Ravana kidnapped Sita. Rama enlisted the help of the super-strong monkey Hanuman and an army of monkeys and bears. They battled Ravana and his demon companions and rescued Sita. Finally, Rama and Sita were allowed to return home. Their friends and relatives lit their way to the palace with divas.

PILGRIMAGE

As well as seasonal celebrations, another special event in Hindu life is *yatra* – pilgrimage. Many Hindus undertake this in later life. It is an opportunity to escape from daily life to focus on spiritual matters and grow closer to God. On pilgrimage, Hindus may bathe in a holy river, visit mandirs or seek spiritual advice from holy people.

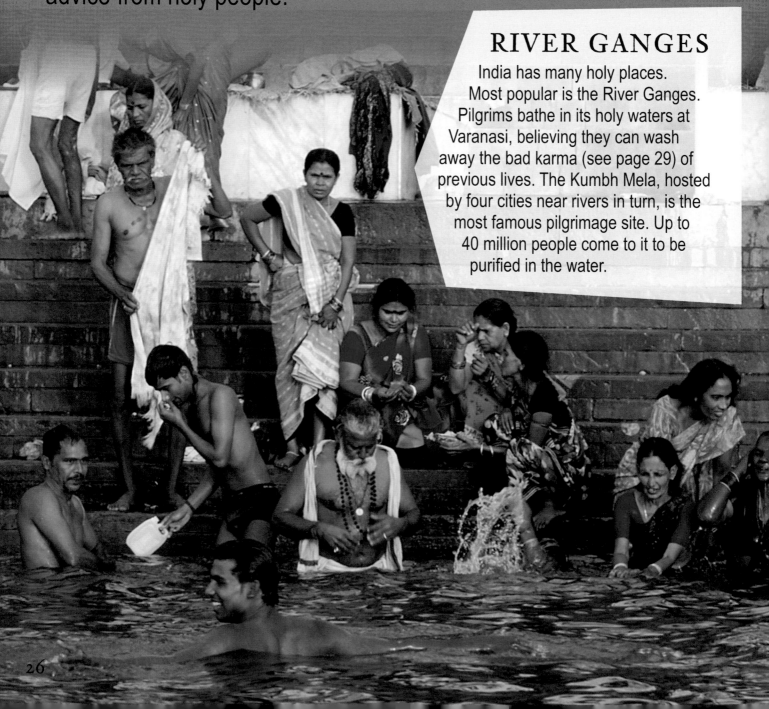

RIVER GANGES

India has many holy places. Most popular is the River Ganges. Pilgrims bathe in its holy waters at Varanasi, believing they can wash away the bad karma (see page 29) of previous lives. The Kumbh Mela, hosted by four cities near rivers in turn, is the most famous pilgrimage site. Up to 40 million people come to it to be purified in the water.

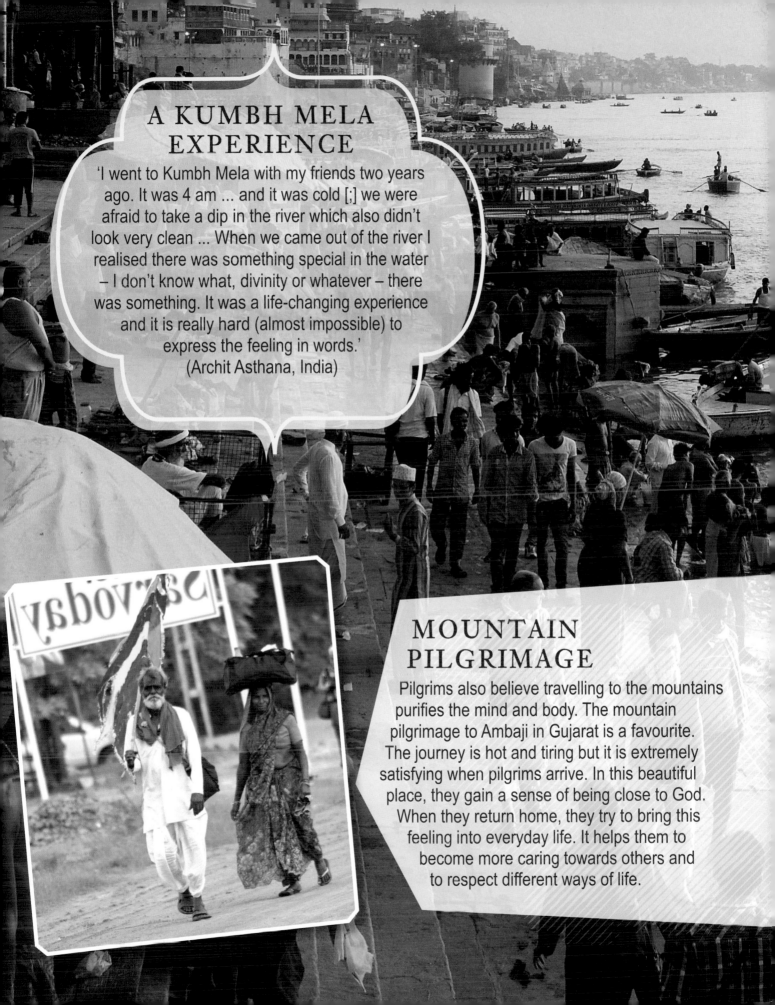

A KUMBH MELA EXPERIENCE

'I went to Kumbh Mela with my friends two years ago. It was 4 am ... and it was cold [;] we were afraid to take a dip in the river which also didn't look very clean ... When we came out of the river I realised there was something special in the water – I don't know what, divinity or whatever – there was something. It was a life-changing experience and it is really hard (almost impossible) to express the feeling in words.'
(Archit Asthana, India)

MOUNTAIN PILGRIMAGE

Pilgrims also believe travelling to the mountains purifies the mind and body. The mountain pilgrimage to Ambaji in Gujarat is a favourite. The journey is hot and tiring but it is extremely satisfying when pilgrims arrive. In this beautiful place, they gain a sense of being close to God. When they return home, they try to bring this feeling into everyday life. It helps them to become more caring towards others and to respect different ways of life.

DEATH – A STAGE IN THE CIRCLE OF LIFE

The last rite of passage marks a person's death. For Hindus, death is not the end. They believe life is a cycle – people are born, die and are born again, perhaps thousands upon thousands of times. Their atman, or real self, simply passes into a different body. This is known as reincarnation. These beliefs can provide comfort in a time of sorrow.

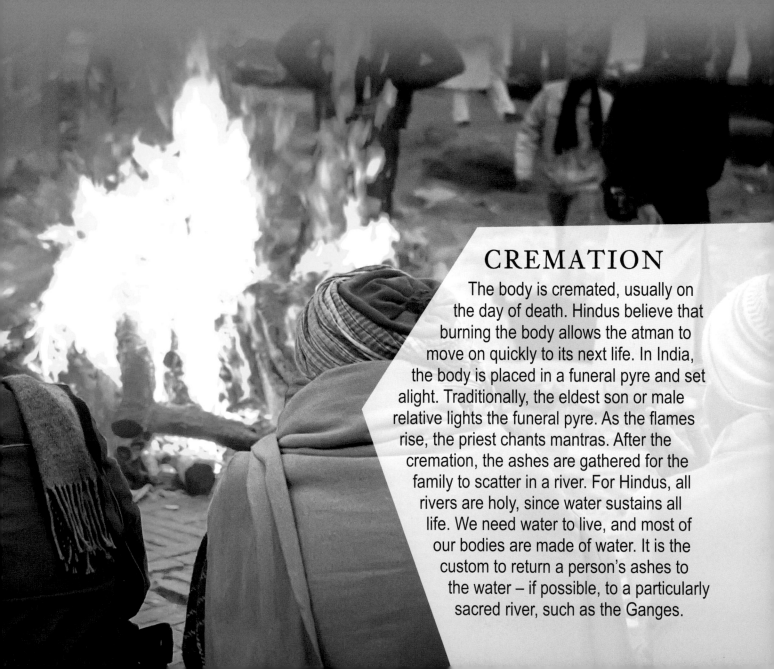

CREMATION

The body is cremated, usually on the day of death. Hindus believe that burning the body allows the atman to move on quickly to its next life. In India, the body is placed in a funeral pyre and set alight. Traditionally, the eldest son or male relative lights the funeral pyre. As the flames rise, the priest chants mantras. After the cremation, the ashes are gathered for the family to scatter in a river. For Hindus, all rivers are holy, since water sustains all life. We need water to live, and most of our bodies are made of water. It is the custom to return a person's ashes to the water – if possible, to a particularly sacred river, such as the Ganges.

IN MOURNING

After the funeral, the family sits in mourning for 10–12 days. Friends and relatives visit each day and bring food. The mourners eat no sweet foods and men do not shave as symbols of grief and respect for the departed soul. Then normal life returns, but a ceremony is held every year to remember the person who has passed away.

KARMA

Hindus believe that the result of your past actions are your *karma*. If you behave well throughout your lifetime, you will have positive karma, and your next life will be good. But you will create bad karma if you are selfish. Hindus hope that if their actions are the best they can be, eventually their karma will be good enough for them to achieve *moksha*, where their atman can reach heaven.

GLOSSARY

arti A welcoming ceremony in which the priest offers the sacred image pure items, such as incense, a lamp and flowers

astrology The study of the positions of the stars and the movements of the planets in the belief that they influence and predict human affairs

atman The real, eternal self, separate from the mind and body.

aum An important Hindu mantra, representing God and the sound at the time of creation. It is often used as the symbol of Hinduism

Brahman The Supreme Being, who resides everywhere and is aware of everything. Some Hindus call Brahman 'God'

chant A prayer with a few words that are said over and over again

cremate To burn a dead body, as part of a funeral ceremony

deity (plural: **deities**) A form of God, or a particular god or goddess

dhal A soup usually made from lentils or split peas

dharma Duty, which helps us to live happily and sustain the world

fast To go without food, sometimes for religious reasons

ghee An oil made from butter, often used in Indian cooking

harmonium A musical instrument like a small organ

honour To show great respect

incense A stick that is burned to give off a nice smell

karma How your actions in this life affect your future in this life and the next

kumkum paste A paste often made from the spice turmeric

lunar calendar A calendar, based on the moon's cycles

mantra A sacred word or prayer that is said again and again. Mantras are important in many Hindu ceremonies.

murti A sacred statue image, usually of God or of a particular god or goddess, used in worship

offering Something such as food or flowers that is offered to the deities on a shrine

pilgrimage A journey to a holy place for religious reasons

prashad Food that is offered to the deities and then shared after worship

priest A person who performs religious duties in the mandir

purity The state of being clean, thinking good thoughts and acting selflessly

pyre Pile of wood on which a dead body is placed and burned

recite To repeat something you have learnt, such as a prayer

reincarnation The idea that, after death, the real self (present in all living beings) enters another body

rite of passage A ceremony or an event that marks an important stage in somebody's life

ritual A series of actions that are always performed in the same way, especially as part of a religious ceremony

sacred Holy – connected with God

sari A long piece of cloth that is wrapped around the body and worn as the main piece of clothing by women from India and other countries in South Asia

scriptures The holy books of a religion

seer A person with great spiritual knowledge

shrine The central, most sacred part of a mandir, which houses the statues. Hindu shrines are also found in homes or outdoors

sitar A traditional stringed instrument

soul A person's real self, which is made up mostly of the mind

spiritual To do with the human mind and feelings, rather than the body, and often used to describe religious feelings

tabla A pair of small drums played with the hands

FIND OUT MORE

Books

Celebrating Hindu Festivals by Liz Miles (Raintree, 2016)

My Hindu Faith by Anita Ganeri (Cherrytree Books, 2015)

We are Hindus by Philip Blake (Franklin Watts, 2015)

A Year of Festivals: Hindu Festivals by Honor Head (Wayland, 2012)

Websites

BBC Bitesize Hinduism Class Clips
www.bbc.com/bitesize/topics/zh86n39/resources/1
Video clips about different aspects of Hindu life

BBC Religions Hinduism
www.bbc.co.uk/religion/religions/hinduism/
A good general introduction to many aspects of Hinduism

Every School Hinduism Religious Education KS2
www.everyschool.co.uk/r-e-key-stage-2-hinduism.html
Introduction to Hinduism and topics including worship,
marriage, Divali, with interactive pages and videos

Hindu Kids Universe
www.hindukidsworld.org/index.php/en/
Aimed at Hindu children, including customs, prayers and stories

Note to parents and teachers:
Every effort has been made by the Publishers to ensure that the websites in this
book are suitable for children, that they are of the highest educational value, and
that they contain no inappropriate or offensive material. However, because of the
nature of the Internet, it is impossible to guarantee that the contents of these sites
will not be altered. We strongly advise that Internet access is supervised by
a responsible adult.

INDEX